SECRET NIL
TECHNIQUES OF

Hakkoryu
Jujutsu

DENNIS PALUMBO

PALADIN PRESS
BOULDER, COLORADO

Other books by Dennis G. Palumbo,
Kaiden Shihan San Dai Kichi:

The Secrets of Hakkoryu Jujutsu: Shodan Tactics

If you have further questions about the techniques and/or training available in Hakkoryu Jujutsu, please do not hesitate to contact the author either through Paladin Press, or at his dojo:

Dennis G. Palumbo
Hakkoryu Martial Arts Federation
12028F East Mississippi Avenue
Aurora, Colorado 80012

Secret Nidan Techniques of Hakkoryu Jujutsu
by Dennis G. Palumbo

Copyright © 1988 by Dennis G. Palumbo

ISBN 0-87364-455-7
Printed in the United States of America

Published by Paladin Press, a division of
Paladin Enterprises, Inc., P.O. Box 1307,
Boulder, Colorado 80306, USA.
(303) 443-7250

Direct inquiries and/or orders to the above address.

Contents

Introduction 1

Chapter 1   **Principles of Self-Defense** 9

Chapter 2   **Walking Exercises** 23

Chapter 3   **Nidan-Gi Waza** 49

Chapter 4   **Origins and Applications of Hakkoryu Waza** 103

Appendix   **Glossary** 127

To Zilie, who gave me everything he ever could, and never asked for anything in return, and Dora, always at his side, supplying the strength for both of us. And to Stephanie and Vincent, the next generation, that they might follow in the steps of their grandparents, with hearts of gold, spirits as strong as steel, and as flexible as the willow tree.

Also to Nidai Soke Okuyama, Ryuho, head of the International Hakkoryu Jujutsu Federation, that he may continue to follow in the footsteps of his father, Dai Soke Okuyama, Ryuho, founder of Hakkoryu. I hope that this book will help make the job of spreading Hakkoryu throughout the world a little easier. Special thanks to Jeff, Al, and the staff and editors of Paladin Press for making this book possible.

In respectful memory of Dai Soke Okyuama (1902–1987) who passed away on 25 November 1987 in Omiya, Japan.

Introduction

Welcome to the world of Hakkoryu jujutsu. Hakkoryu jujutsu is a Japanese martial art which utilizes bending of human joints to subdue attackers. The name Hakkoryu means "School of Eight Lights" in keeping with Dai Soke Okyuama's belief that the color spectrum as we know it is made up of nine bands of light. The eighth band, a very weak but still extant color, a shade of red, remains in the background and receives its power from the ninth color, purple. Since one of the underlying principles and philosophies of Hakkoryu jujutsu is that the practitioner remain calm, unobtrusive, and "in the background" of situations—using his skills only as a last resort to protect himself, loved ones, or others—this term aptly identifies one of the basic tenets of training in Hakkoryu jujutsu.

This book on nidan techniques, or the second level of training in Hakkoryu jujutsu, describes more advanced tactics than those of the book entitled *The Secrets of Hakkoryu Jujutsu: Shodan Tactics.* The techniques of nidan build directly upon the techniques of shodan, and the first book should definitely be referred to before beginning or continuing to study from this volume. As in the first book, in which there were specific principles which were basic to mastery of

1

shodan tactics or waza, the group of principles presented here are specifically dedicated to nidan level waza. The primary principles of nidan waza are the following: nidan wrist bend; *matsuba dori* (pine-needle break); *konoha gaeshi* (turning of the leaf); *maki komi* (wrapping technique); *aya dori* (woven-art technique); and *shuto jime* (sword-hand lock principle).

You will notice that many of the techniques in this book have similar names, as is the procedure with Hakkoryu. However, each technique is itself different, based on the level of application. For example, a *shodan ude osae dori* (sleeve grab defense) of the shodan level is performed quite differently in the nidan level, even though it has the same name for the basic waza. Keep this point in mind, so as not to confuse yourself in practice.

At the nidan level, Dai Soke Okuyama (the founder of Hakkoryu) defines the skill level of the practitioner as:

> . . . a student who is capable of practicing more freely with a partner in order to discover the sense of combat and the different aspects of immediate defense. He is capable of applying all the basic techniques at normal speed. This is the level of [the] technician, who is no longer just a student.

As such, the student has the increased responsibility of ensuring that his or her practice partner is not injured during training. The techniques of nidan are in many cases easier to execute than in shodan, and they are in most cases even more painful than those of shodan. Therefore execute extreme care while practicing these nidan-level techniques so as not to inadvertently injure your partner.

The major key to nidan waza, both in execution and reception, is to relax as much as possible. When applying the techniques, one must avoid the tendency to tighten up the muscles of the arms and shoulders when performing the techniques, and must concentrate his mind on the *tanden*[1]. When performing the exercises in *seiza*[2], remember always to keep from upsetting your own balance while defending against the attacks of *kake*[3].

In addition to the new techniques of nidan, you will also be introduced to eight nidan walking-exercise sets designed to prepare the student to defend against attacks from the rear, kicks, and close or surprise attacks to the upper body. These exercises are illustrated in "bunkai" application (i.e., with a partner) in order to more fully demonstrate their application and use.

Many of the techniques will also be illustrated in their "street application" outside of the dojo, so as to present them in an arena of practical reference and possible application if the need arises.

Remember to practice slowly and diligently, paying close attention to your actions. Realize full well that many of these techniques, if used too forcefully or in the wrong hands for the wrong reasons, can cause very serious pain, and, in some cases, permanent damage to an assailant. If you keep these points in mind while practicing, you will soon develop the confidence to know you need not react violently to every threatening situation that might present itself. You will learn to keep your composure, responding only when you feel it is absolutely necessary, and then doing so with power, control, and efficiency.

NIDAN ADVANCEMENT

When you have devoted the time necessary to the study and mastery of nidan level techniques (waza), you deserve to know what you can expect of yourself. In the study of nidan, it is imperative that the student learn to relax and begin to develop the quiet confidence of his abilities. By learning to relax during practice, the student will soon be able to increase his or her threshold of pain tolerance. Techniques which may have been extremely painful during the learning

---

[1] The area considered to be in the *hara* (stomach), three to five inches below the navel and the center of all bodily power.

[2] The formal kneeling or sitting position for practicing.

[3] The term used in Hakkoryu to describe the attacker or aggressor (similar to uke, or fall guy, in other arts).

of shodan should be much more easily tolerated with less discomfort and as a result of studying nidan. The student will learn to absorb the pain of various locks and binds and shrug off the resultant pain. By learning to breathe properly (i.e., exhaling strongly from the tanden at the first sign of pain from a lock), and relaxing by actually attempting to bend the joint being locked in the same direction, the student will be well on the way to mastering most situations he might find himself encountering. In time, this will transfer to the student's attitude of overall self-defense awareness. He will learn to relax more quickly so that, when faced with a potentially threatening situation, his response is more natural, spontaneous, and effective.

More specifically, the student will learn:

The extremely versatile principle and technique of *shiho nage*

The powerful applications of konoha gaeshi

The excruciating pain of the nidan wrist locks and control pins

The deceptively effective applications of the maki komi principle

The pressure point pin of *te kagami*

The painful, disabling thumb break technique of matsuba dori

The one-hand defensive locks and escapes of shuto jime

Basic defense against two attackers

Defense against rear attacks and grabs in street-fighting situations

Defenses against front kicks

Defense against the up-close sucker punch attack.

Additionally, the student will be prepared to defend against the barroom idiot looking to pick a fight for nothing. You'll learn how to defend against attacks while sitting in a chair; defenses against the chest grabs and strikes; defense against attacks in close quarters; and defense from pulling attacks, such as theft of your briefcase or purse while walking. All these things and more can be accomplished when you take the time to master nidan tactics.

Historically, the techniques of nidan are some of the most painful in the style of Hakkoryu Jujutsu. They place great stress and pain on the joints of the wrists, elbows, and shoulders. Without much additional pressure, a controlling technique can easily be turned into an extremely destructive technique. It is only in life-threatening situations, however, that the Hakkoryu practitioner is morally justified in taking his techniques to this extreme. In the overwhelming majority of situations in which the student might find himself, the basic controls and submissions of Hakkoryu will more than suffice to nullify the danger of the situation and render the assailant helpless.

In the olden days of karate on Okinawa, Japan, many of the masters required the new students to literally break their knuckles in the first few days of training to develop calcium deposits when the knuckles healed. The new students would then rebreak their knuckles to enhance the result, creating over a period of time a *seiken* (forefist) of almost solid calcium deposits, with the first two knuckles being virtually welded together, able to deliver a devastating strike with a single blow.

The techniques of old jujutsu were in some instances just as inhumane. It was not uncommon for new students, or *shoshinsha,* to be initiated into the dojo the first day or night in class by being the *uke,* or fall guy, for the senior student or instructor. The uke would be bounced off the tatami or wooden floor like a ball, and techniques would be applied to him that would either break or severely damage the wrists, arms, and ligaments of the joints. Much of this initiation was done to weed out the serious student from the casual observer. Many times, the only reason it was done was because the senior students and instructors had each experienced the initiation, and this was the way they passed it on to the new students. If you couldn't take it, you would leave. And if you survived and still wanted to learn, it was just a preview of what the training would be like. Fortunately, those days have passed, and that hard-core attitude is rarely seen in legitimate dojos today.

I remember the evening I took my black belt examination in Shudokan Karate in Fussa City, Japan. The exam was, as expected, quite thorough and demanding, but I felt that I had done well that Friday evening, and though rather tired and a little bruised from the sparring, etc., I felt quite good about the results. After the examination, the presentation of awards was set for the following Friday evening. When I showed up that next Friday with the two other individuals who had also tested the previous week, my sensei introduced me to a visitor from Tokyo, the head of the Shudokan school who had come for the presentation. As the ceremonies progressed, it was finally time to receive my black belt. I assumed, correctly, that I would receive my belt from my sensei. However, I then received another belt from the dojo headmaster, Toshio Hanaue—my senior sensei—and the confusion began. To top it off, the visitor from Tokyo called me up and presented me with a third black belt. I was honored, confused, curious, and mystified.

The implications of what had occurred didn't strike me until the end of the presentation, when Sensei said that the new black belts should be sure to come to class the next evening, Saturday, with their new belts on. Which belt did I dare wear to class? Were I to wear the belt my instructor gave me, I would be causing great embarrassment to the senior instructor who had also given me a belt. If I wore the belt of my senior instructor, I would be slighting the head of the system who had traveled from Tokyo for the presentation and also presented me with a belt—let alone my own instructor who, as a sixth dan black belt, was now on the bottom of the totem pole. If I wore the belt of the visitor from Tokyo, I would be causing my senior instructor to lose face by not wearing his belt. What to do? I won't reveal my solution to the dilemma; rather, I leave the mystery to the reader to try to figure out what he or she might have done in this situation.

After arriving at the dojo on Saturday evening, and while changing into my uniform, I noticed a few new faces among the black belts who I had not seen before. I also noticed that there were no *mudansha* (individuals below the rank of black belt) in the changing room. I figured they may have already moved into the dojo and were warming up. To my surprise, when I and the other two new *yudansha* (black belts) entered the dojo to get ready for practice, there were no colored belts in the dojo—only black belts, twelve of them not counting we three new ones. After a few minutes of warm-ups and stretching, the senior instructor said that tonight would be a night to "honor" the new black belts in class, and that we would have the honor of sparring against each of the other black belts present, starting with the lowest ranking—a nidan—and working up to the senior ranking—a *shichidan* (seventh dan).

Misery. To try to explain the pain and humiliation of fighting so many people, and such varied levels of experience would be moot. By the time we each were able to fight the seventh dan, standing was a painful experience, let alone fighting. Suffice it to say, the shichidan proceeded ceremoniously to wipe the dojo floor with us, easily and thoroughly. It was our initiation into the yudansha ranks, and the experience served to remind us that the shiny new black belt we had just received meant only that we were still only "beginners." It did more than give us some bruises—it made us realize what *humble* really meant. There's nothing like a good thrashing to bring a new black belt back down to earth. When it was all over, my dojo master, Toshio Hanaue Sensei, came up to each of us, smiled, and said, "Congratulations— and welcome to the dojo." I think it was worth it after all!

At the Hakkoryu Hombu (headquarters) in Japan, the "humility" lesson is somewhat different, especially if you are a *gaijin*, or foreigner. For new students the training is quite gentle in the application of techniques in order not to cause any unnecessary injury which might discourage the student. At the higher levels, however, when a *sandan* or *yondan* (third or fourth degree black belt) comes to the Hombu to train and review his techniques, possibly in preparation for *shihan*, or master instructor, training, he is expected to have perfected the techniques of his level. Sometimes while practicing and exchanging techniques with one of the senior instructors, should a yudansha do a technique incorrectly, the senior instructor will avoid saying anything to correct him. He will merely ask the student to repeat the same attack that he just made. The instructor will then reapply the technique or waza. But when he applies the technique, it is done perfectly, and somehow his hearing seems to falter momentarily—you are tapping on the mat, yelling "Itai!," trying to get him to stop the pain, and he just doesn't seem to hear you at all. Having thus been shown the correct technique, when you next perform the technique on the instructor, to show him that you understand, it had better be right. If not, he will "courteously" demonstrate it to you once again—with an even greater loss of hearing than the first time. If you haven't caught on after one or two of these demonstrations, you're in deep trouble. As my father used to say, "It's like hitting your head against a brick wall—it feels good when you stop." When you stop trying to prove you know it all, it all works.

There is no malice involved in this type of practice. It's merely a way of showing the student that whatever he's doing can be done even better. It must be true, because it feels so good when the instructor stops!

I hope that these short anecdotes will impress upon you the importance of realizing that no matter how much you know, there is always more you can learn—not only about the style or system you study, but about yourself. Always keep this in mind when you train. Be courteous to your dojo mates. Train hard, sweat, ache, repeat, hurt, and love it. Every time you finish a class or a practice session, you should ask yourself what you learned. If you didn't learn anything, either in technique or about yourself, then you just wasted one-and-a-half or two hours. You could have been out jogging or playing golf instead. Each time you train, you should learn *something,* or you're wasting your time.

Chapter 1

Principles of Self-Defense

To become a master of Hakkoryu, the student must develop the attitude of *Hakko-botsunyu;* That is, to be devoted and sink into Hakkoryu, to be engrossed fully in Hakkoryu. Then, as Dai Soke Okuyama says, the power of even one waza conquers as the divine punishes his aggressor *(ichigi-hitchu).*

Since self-protection and self-defense are subjects of major concern among many individuals engaged in the study of the martial arts, I feel that some basic principles outlining overall attitudes of training and practice should be mentioned for those who may not be aware of the difference between just going through the motions of training, and worthwhile training and the effective use of time.

PRINCIPLES

The major principles I feel each individual should incorporate into his or her training are listed below and can apply to all levels of training, from beginner to advanced practitioner.

Stance

Use the basic T-stance, or *teiji-dachi,* with a little more than half of your weight on the rear leg and the back foot turned at a 45-degree angle. This is a natural stance and does not convey to an attacker that you have had any special training. Remember that dropping into a standard or rigid formal stance as your first action has already eliminated the element of surprise which is so important to success and victory.

Balance

Keep the knees slightly flexed at all times—do not lock the knees. Keep your center of gravity as low as possible in the pelvic region, tucking the buttocks in and concentrating on the hara and tanden within.

Deflection

When possible, do not attempt to block a blow or strike to your body with direct force. Learn to deflect and/or redirect the blow through a combination of body positioning *(tai sabaki),* hand movement, balance, and footwork.

Smoothness

When practicing the nidan techniques, repeat them so that the actions become one continuous, smooth movement—not jerky and forced. This fluidity will come only through repeated practice of the basics.

Transition

Through frequent and continual practice of basic techniques, you will be able to move from one technique to a second or third, or more if necessary. If a particular technique does not work the way you want it to, discard it *immediately,* and move rapidly to another technique or principle without hesitation.

Follow-through

Once an action or reaction has begun, follow through completely to the finish—don't hesitate, stop, or reconsider your actions. Your response must be spontaneous, proper, thorough, and complete. This is especially true in training. If you get in the bad practice of doing a technique only half-heartedly or not finishing the technique, when the time comes for you to react to a life-threatening situation, your response can only be the same—half way.

Control

After completing a technique, maintain full control of the individual until you are satisfied he or she is no longer a threat. Whether this control be by holding the opponent in a submission hold or lock, or in the case of a police officer, by handcuffing, you must make this determination yourself.

Self-Confidence

Through continual practice you *will* develop the self-confidence to handle most situations with little or no difficulty. Each time you do, this will again reinforce and build your confidence.

> You must be deadly serious in training. When I say that, I do not mean that you should not be reasonably diligent or moderately in earnest. I mean that your opponent must always be present in your mind, whether you sit or stand, or walk or raise your arms.
> Funakoshi, Gichin

THE ATTITUDE OF TRAINING

The instructor instructs, the students obey,
   who is the teacher and who the students?
The warrior priest, living in the temple,
   walks alone without fear.

The ronin wanders, throughout the land searching,

for glorious deeds to do.
I strike the makiwara, the mind and the punch are one,
  what is there to seek?
My students practice, together and alone,
  neither one nor the other I practice kumite,
  the attack and the defense are one,
  what is there to learn?

                                                    Zen story

As you begin your training, there are some points that you must keep in mind as part of the training. Aside from the more obvious ones of learning a technique, a specific stance, or hand position, these points have more to do with you and your partner's attitudes during training. In order for both of you to get the most out of your training, these points must be kept uppermost in the mind.

First, walk through the new techniques one at a time, slowly, with your partner. Do not attempt to do them quickly, or to change them. Remember, these waza are based on proven techniques and principles, developed over centuries, and, in many cases, tempered in the fire of combat by people who had to use them to save their lives or the lives of their loved ones. Do not, in your naiveté, attempt to improve on the skill and experience of masters who devised the techniques.

Second, the partner, or *kake,* should not attempt to resist the technique, nor should he anticipate the result of the technique. Instead, he should cooperate with the *tori,* who performs the waza, to better facilitate understanding and learning of the waza. There is nothing to prove by resisting a technique, especially when you know what the technique is. Almost anyone can avoid or resist a technique if he knows in advance what it will be—no surprise there!

Third, do *not* rely on brute force to perform a technique properly and get the desired result. The difference between the proper execution of a principle or technique and the use of brute force is just that—technique. If the principle is not fully understood and performed slowly at first, mistakes will be made that are counterproductive to learning and will make all applications futile.

Fourth, after practicing slowly and getting a "feel" for the technique, gradually increase the speed of execution and the control element of the particular technique. At this time, the partner (kake) may begin using a slight amount of resistance to make the technique more realistic, if desired.

Fifth, when the partners feel comfortable with a particular technique, you can begin experimenting with different applications of the principle involved, but only with the approval of the head instructor. This does not mean changing the basic waza; it means the application, or *tekiyo,* of a particular waza to a slightly different situation.

Finally, if a particular technique is not working the way it should, resist the temptation to force it by using excessive power. Stop, find the error, and try to correct the technique rather than take a chance on hurting your practice partner. Remember that courtesy in the dojo is much more than just saying "Thank you."

THEORY OF TRAINING IN NIDAN-GI

The nidan, or second level of training in Hakkoryu, differs from the shodan and upper levels of training in more than just waza. To further explain these differences, I offer the definition of the differences as explained by Dai Soke Okuyama.

In Japan, since tradition is still respected, the masters of many schools of jujutsu define the value of the grades which are the end products of a progression correctly learned in the following way:

First dan indicates a student who has all the basics necessary for his evolution toward becoming expert in the art. In fact, though he knows very few applications, he has sufficiently prepared his body to undergo them. This is the true level of the student who is no longer a neophyte.

Second dan indicates a student who is capable of practicing more freely with a partner in order to discover the sense of combat and the different aspects of immediate defense.

He is capable of applying all the basic techniques at normal, quick speed. This is the level of the technician *(ko),* who is no longer a mere student.

The third dan black belt is a student who, assuredly, is capable of confronting several adversaries concurrently. He executes the techniques with more speed, precision, and power. Moreover, he has been initiated to different sensitive and pain points located on the meridians of the heart and other internal organs. This is the true level of a practitioner who is more than just a technician.

The fourth dan is a student capable of controlling several kinds of attacks, with his arms, in different circumstances. He has been initiated as to the different pressure points which are along the median adjoining the lungs and the heart. This is the level at which one is already considered an expert in Japan.

As a fifth dan, a student is capable of mastering his techniques and applying them without harming others in training sessions. In the opinion of the masters, this is the highest level in the technical grades, which means that one has reached his maximum potential on the physical level. It is after this attainment and demonstration of ability that the individual is allowed to enter into training for shihan (master instructor), with a beginning of the esoteric and medical knowledge of the system and the *okuden* (the secret techniques).

As Dai Soke Okuyama, Ryuho, would often mention in his writings and lectures, it is important to remember that to obtain the first dan is not sufficient in itself. In fact, numerous other techniques are taught beyond this basic level. Thus, at the time of the exam, the student is not interrogated solely on the practicality of the techniques. The instructor judges essentially on the whole of the candidate's behavior and demands the immediate application of one or several techniques on demand, regardless of which attack or grab is used. The instructor and judges look for calmness, quickness of execution, precision of technique, body stability, everything executed with minimum effort and maximum efficiency . . . that's what a person who holds the grade of black belt should be able to do. The instructor, like-wise, pays close attention to the candidate's state of mind; his attitude toward the instructor, judges, the masters, and the upper and lower grades. In a word, *sonkei*—respect. Any absence of respect or any show of brutality, as well as any hesitation at the time of applying a technique, can bring about an annulment of the black belt grade. This is the rea-son the exam doesn't last very long. In twenty to thirty min-utes the value of a student can be determined.

Like all methods of jujutsu in Japan, the techniques of Hakkoryu are based on the possibility of rendering an assail-ant unable to do any harm in a minimum amount of time and effort. As the masters proclaim, in such a case, no hesi-tation is permitted. "It is an *instant* of truth between life—which is short—and death—which is long."

The levels of training beyond fourth dan include the fol-lowing ranks, or titles: *shihan, renshi shihan, shihan menkyo kaiden (kaiden shihan),* and the last and highest ranking awarded to practitioners of Hakkoryu, *san dai kichu* (three great foundation pillars). This last rank is the equivalent of the eighth dan.

In most cases, the testing for shihan and higher levels is done in Japan, at the Hakkoryu Zenkoku Shihan Kai-Hakko-juku Hombu. For a student to be permitted to train or be permitted to begin training for senior ranks at the Hombu, he must be recommended by a bona fide shihan, or higher rank, to the Hombu. One cannot just drop in to train or test. The Hombu is a private school (Hakkojuku) for the advanced training of its senior disciples. The testing for the senior grades such as shihan begins on the eighth day of each month and lasts approximately two weeks. If the candidate is succesful, he or she will be awarded the rank and title of shihan in the Bugei art of Hakkoryu jujutsu—an accomplish-ment certainly to be proud of, and one not easily attained.

I felt especially proud of this accomplishment in Novem-ber 1963, when I arrived in Tokyo with my instructor, Abukawa Shihan, to begin my training for the shihan level, during a cold winter. My instructor, who had accompanied me for the training and to act as interpreter for me, mentioned how happy he was to be taking me to the Hombu for this training. He also mentioned how cold it was and would be in the Hombu, since there was no heat other than that provided by small hibachi heaters under the tables. How cold could it get, really? From where I had just come, the northernmost tip of Japan, Wakkanai on Hakkaido, we had experienced snow drifts fifteen to twenty feet high. But the cold was understandable, and we were ready for it.

Lesson number one: never underestimate your environment! When it was time to get up for breakfast the next morning, after sleeping under two feet of futon covers which raised my body temperature to a comfortable 98 degrees-plus, I was a bit more than surprised when Sensei said, *"Ikimasho* ("let's go")! I jumped out of bed, and was bitten by the stabbing ice-cold wind whipping through the wide-open, sliding windows of the upstairs sleeping area of the Hombu. It was a comfortable 31 degrees (ha!), and time to begin cleaning *(niten soji),* washing, and wiping down everything in the room in preparation for breakfast. Finally, after about thirty minutes of vigorous cleaning—more in an effort to warm up than because of unbridled enthusiasm—we had finished the niten soji, and my appetite for a good hearty breakfast began to build. I was drinking some warm green tea, visualizing the massive breakfast I was going to devour.

Lesson number two: the Japanese don't eat as big breakfasts as we had had in the U.S. armed services, and they certainly didn't eat the same type of food served in the army mess halls. We finally received the call from Soke's wife to come down and eat. I sat down to two small bowls, one with rice, the other with some spiced vegetables, and a *raw* egg. No fried eggs, no toast, no coffee—how will I survive this two weeks on such paltry fare, I wondered. Mrs. Okuyama soon saw the dismay on my face and asked me if I wasn't hungry. I said, "Yes," but I didn't think this would be enough for me. She brought me another raw egg and more vegetables. Finally, my sensei said that I might lose face if I didn't eat the breakfast she had prepared for me, so I'd better eat it. I was more worried about losing something worse than face!

Just as I had broken the first egg and poured some *shoyu* (soy sauce) over it, Mrs. Okuyama came back into the dining area with a beautiful pair of fried eggs and two large pieces of toast, with a big smile on her face. I thanked her profusely, thanked the "spirits" for intervening, and dug into the best looking pair of sunnyside-up eggs I'd ever seen!

Returning to the original topic of this section, I want to impress upon you the mental state you should have when studying the nidan waza. First, as a part of your regular practice sessions, you should not forget to practice and review often the waza of shodan. As mentioned earlier, these new nidan techniques, in many cases, build directly on the basic techniques of shodan, and to disregard the earlier level would be incorrect. As you progress in your training, you will see that you can easily switch from a nidan to a shodan technique quite effortlessly, and this type of transition should be carefully noted and practiced after mastering the basic waza of nidan individually. Do not rush to be able to combine these varied waza. Rather, let it come naturally and spontaneously. When you can go from one technique to another without thinking, you will be well on your way to success!

The next area of importance is to not concern yourself with analyzing each technique in detail. In the words of Dai Soke Okuyama, the founder of Hakkoryu, you should merely attempt "to get the feel of the technique, and relax." I cannot overemphasize the idea of relaxation during performance and training with these waza. Stiffness and rigidity will cause soreness and pain that may last for an extended period after training. If you find that you are having some soreness and lingering pain, this, in most cases, can be attributed to tenseness and stiffness during training—avoid rigidity whenever possible. To do this, concentrate on your tanden during the entire execution of the technique, and on nothing else.

The techniques of nidan place quite a bit of stress on the wrist joints, tendons, and surrounding ligaments, and the pain felt during application or receipt of these waza is very sharp. For this reason, the student should attempt to increase the range of flexibility in his wrists—forward, backward, and to the sides.

At the Hombu, in Japan, students are very often reminded of the importance of using the little-finger side of the hand. This is often emphasized when doing such simple things as picking up a glass of water. The student is reminded to hold the glass with the last two fingers of the hand, and to relax and point the index finger. Many of the shihan have made a practice game of testing each other's strength in their grip by locking the little fingers of one hand and trying to throw or pull the other across the dojo floor using the little-finger grip alone. One of the most formidable proponents of this exercise, however, is Kaiden Shihan San Dai Kichu Yashuhiro Irie, head instructor at the Hombu, and longtime student and childhood friend of Nidai Soke Okuyama, Rhuho.

The instructor learns from teaching,
The students learn from being taught,
Who is the student, and who the Master?

THE CONCEPT OF DEFENSE IN HAKKORYU

The concept of self-protection in Hakkoryu is based on a number of principles, not the least of which is the utilization of *atemi-waza* (strikes to the vital points of the body). Interestingly enough, these same vital points used as a part of the self-defense aspect of Hakkoryu are also used to treat the body to recover from pain and illness, and promote good health. When used in this manner, the techniques of *koho igaku shiatsu* (imperial way of finger pressure massage) come into play. As an example, the lung meridian point on the inside of the wrist is a very painful and powerful atemi point when pressure is applied, and can bring a person to his knees immediately, screaming in pain. Depending upon the amount of pressure utilized on this point, such a technique can cause a person to lose consciousness and/or be temporarily paralyzed. However, this same point, in a similar application, can promote proper breathing and can be used to help a person recover from hyperventilation and rapid breathing. The dual path of Hakkoryu is fascinating to say the least, and it requires many years of study to become knowledgeable in both paths. For the average person, the learning of the jujutsu and self-protection portions of the art is more than enough for his individual needs and requirements. But it is, it should be remembered, only one side of the coin.

The techniques of Hakkoryu are, for the most part, based on defenses against attacks that were prevalent in days past, against grappling attacks, sword attacks, etc. A basic defensive technique against the well-known *oi zuki*, or thrusting punch, is an application derived from earlier attacks with a tanto or other short-bladed weapon. Karate, as an empty-hand form of self-defense, is relatively young in its history. The waza of Hakkoryu are specifically designed to provide defense against attacks from the front, rear, sides, and above. Utilizing the basic principles involved in learning the specific waza for these types of attacks, the practitioner can easily adapt to variations in attack, whether it be from a different angle, or utilizing a weapon as part of the attack.

The types of attacks that Hakkoryu concerns itself with are the grab, strike, thrust, kick, and those utilizing weapons. Included in each of these categories, of course, are variations on these types of attacks. The grab may be single-handed on the wrist, shoulder, chest, from the side, the rear, around the arms, under the arms, around the waist, around the neck, etc. The strike may be a punch straight to the body, a round-house strike to the head *(yoko men uchi),* an uppercut, a punch from the side, or it may be combined with a particular type of grab described earlier. The thrust may be open-handed, with a stick, knife, sword, long stick, or pole. The kick may be a front kick, roundhouse kick, rear thrust, side thrust, etc.

At this point, however, it should be noted that traditional jujutsu was not designed to defend against karate. This is for various reasons. First, there was no such thing as karate when jujutsu and aiki-jujutsu were in their heyday of development. The fighting·was of a combat, grappling, and defense-against-weapons nature—a *life-threatening* nature. Secondly, just as jujutsu arts are not designed to defend against karate-type arts, the opposite is equally true. Karate arts are not designed to defend against jujutsu-type arts.

One of the most common things I notice when teaching seminars to individuals, especially black belt instructors of various karate-type arts, is their lack of defensive abilities against the grappling arts. If he is two to three feet away from you, the karate fighter might be able to kick you to pieces, but when you put him in a close-quarter encounter, he invariably becomes confused, strained, and frustrated in his attempts to extricate himself. The thing I find most interesting, however, is that almost all karate-type arts, though they may begin with basics of kicking, striking, blocking, and punching, evolve at the higher levels into close-quarter defenses of jujutsu. Most such defenses are rather crude, and the emphasis is rarely on principles to be learned and employed, but, nevertheless, they eventually evolve to this state of self-defense.

One of the beauties of the jujutsu and aiki-jujutsu arts is they allow the practitioner a total range of responses from the very subtle to the very violent, depending on the situation at hand. The karate arts, on the other hand, usually respond in a uniform manner—the full-power, knockdown, put-him-out response. Although there is not a specific waza in Hakkoryu for a defense against a karate kick, any experienced jujutsu practitioner should easily be able to apply the principles of deflection, body movement *(tai sabaki),* and atemi, in response to a kick, without the slightest hesitation. The principles are the same; only the type of attack changes.

Another category of attacks is weapons attacks. Whether the weapon is a stick, long staff, short stick, knife, or sword, the principles learned in the basic waza apply universally. The principles of Hakkoryu allow the individual facing a weapon attack to do various things. He can block the attack, neutralize the attack, thwart the attack, counterattack simultaneously when there is a *suki* (gap), turn the attacker's weapon against him, contain the attacker's weapon, extricate the attacker's weapon, or knock the weapon completely from the control of the attacker. All of these possibilities exist within the realm of the nidan techniques of Hakkoryu. None are beyond the ability of the average practitioner, possibly only beyond his enthusiasm. The intensity of the student determines how soon, if ever, he will become able to perform in such a manner. However, all the tools are there, and the foundation is set. It is up to the student, to use an analogy, whether he wants to build a house of poor quality or a mansion of which to be proud.

The last area that nidan deals with is in the realm of defense against multiple attackers. In many cases, this situation is ideal for application of the *hakko no kamae* (stance of Hakkoryu) known as *senpenbanka,* or stance of innumerable changes (literally one thousand times ten thousand positions). One of the primary principles of defense against multiple attackers is to concentrate your attention closely on only one of the attackers—normally on the leader of the group, if he leads the group. By concentrating your moves against this individual, you can turn him against the others who will be unable to attack simultaneously because of the nature of a simultaneous attack: they get in each other's way, and none can make an effective single attack. Understanding this simple secret can make the difference immediately between victory and defeat. This will be revealed to you if you practice earnestly.

Aiki is to defeat your opponent with a single glance.
Sokaku Takeda

Chapter 2

Walking Exercises

The walking exercises used by the Hakkoryu Martial Arts Federation (HMAF) have been developed to provide the student with practice in movements of reaction and defense from varied situations. All of these numbered exercises are "four count," and can and should be practiced interchangeably with other walking exercises learned to date, in random fashion. An example of practicing these exercises randomly is, from a standing position, to merely announce out loud any three walking exercises you have learned, in any order, and perform them without thinking of their movements; announce, e.g., 5, 8, 6A—all done immediately after the announcement. At first this may cause many to stop and think of what to do in each exercise, but you must strive to overcome that tendency and start immediately to execute the walking exercises announced. As you continue to do this, you will begin to respond spontaneously to the exercise numbers called. You will merely react to each number called without having to think of the response, thus paving the way to a more spontaneous, intuitive reaction.

When performing these walking exercises, do not attempt to perform them as quickly as you can. Any speed applied should come naturally as geared to the intended technique,

not just for speed's sake. The same holds especially true
for the waza as you learn them. Speed will come automa-
tically after you have mastered the principle and waza involved. Always keep in mind the specific principle you are
learning, because these principles will eventually allow you
to devise applications of the basic waza for varied circumstances.

For the most part, the stances used in nidan waza are the
same as those used in shodan, emphasizing, again, the use of
the Teiji- or T-dachi stance for standing techniques, and the
seiza (kneeling) and *hantachi* (kneeling, one knee raised)
position for the kneeling techniques. It should be remembered that the learning of the basic waza in the seiza position is to facilitate concentration of the hand technique
involved, and to strengthen the hips and knees. Any technique done in seiza can easily be applied to a sitting situation in a chair.

These walking exercises were developed to teach the
student's body a variety of things, first of which is *kame,*
and movement of the body from the hips, with emphasis on
the tanden and the hara. This is most important in effective
movement of the tori (the defender), either in evading or
applying techniques, especially against multiple attackers.
The second thing learned in those exercises which involve
rolls, either forward or backward, is a bit of *shiatsu* (massage)
therapy performed on the body by the student's rolling over
certain meridians of the body, thus stimulating blood flow
and providing energy for the upcoming training session. The
third thing the body learns is the importance of a body
warm-up period before practice, which helps to relieve any
stiffness in the joints, tension, and tiredness before beginning
practice. Warm-ups can and should be performed regularly,
both before and after practice if time permits.

BUNKAI OF WALKING EXERCISES

The nidan walking exercises are numbered 5 through 8,
and 5A through 8A. Though Exercise 5 is the first in the
nidan level, this numbering system is spread throughout the

black-belt levels of Hakkoryu Jujutsu. In fact, exercises 1 through 4 and 1A through 4A are shodan walking exercises, and the exercises numbered higher than Exercise 8A are revealed through mastering the higher levels of Hakkoryu. Refer to these exercises as 5 through 8 and 5A through 8A and you will be studying the secrets of Hakkoryu as are Hakkoryu black belts around the world.

The nidan Exercise 5 is designed to condition the tori (student being attacked) to respond correctly to an attacker who might be grabbing his sleeve from the rear, pulling him around, and attempting to strike him. Tori, facing forward, turns to the rear, while sliding away slightly from the direction of the attacker. He turns with his arm held firm, hand open, makes a downward deflection followed by a *metsubushi* (open-handed strike to face), then steps through with his rear leg, and pushes toward kake's chin. Tori follows through again, pushing on kake's chin, then pivots back, and finishes the exercises. Remember that all walking exercises end facing the same direction in which they begin.

Tori is grabbed from the rear with an inside grab and pulled around; kake attempts to strike him in the midsection (Photos 1 and 2). Tori then deflects the strike downward with his right hand (Photo 3), and immediately steps through, pushing kake back with two full push-aways in the senpenbanka stance (Photos 4 through 6).

Photo 1

Photo 2

Photo 3

Photo 4

Photo 5

Photo 6

Exercise 6 begins with tori standing in the T-dachi stance, but this time he is grabbed from the outside by his attacker (i.e., the attacker grabs his right arm with his right hand, and attempts to turn him around and strike him). Tori turns, sliding slightly away from the kake, with his arm held firmly, and simultaneously executes a middle knuckle atemi to the ribs of the kake. Tori then executes a forward shoulder roll to escape. After the roll, he stands and repeats the movement to his rear again, and recovers facing in the same direction.

In Photos 7 through 10, tori is again grabbed from the rear in an outside grab. He turns quickly, keeping his arm firm, and thus keeping the attacker from striking him with his left hand. He then performs an escape roll away over his right shoulder, and recovers behind the attacker. Note that, in a multiple-attacker situation or a life-threatening scenario, tori might possibly roll into the side of the leg of the attacker, thus dislocating his knee, and preventing kake from attacking further.

Photo 7

Photo 8

Photo 9

Photo 10

Exercise 7 deals with a defense against a front thrust or groin kick. Tori begins with a T-dachi stance. He steps out with his lead leg, and performs an inside-out scooping block with his hand, keeping his hand hooked to hold the kicking leg. He then performs a palm heel strike to the nose of kake, his hand grabbing the attacker's hair, pulling down as his knee strikes to the solar plexus of the attacker, knocking out kake's wind, and he steps forward with the kicking leg. Tori finishes by taking one more step forward to end the exercise.

In Photos 11 through 16, tori defends against a front kick by scooping the kick to the outside, grabbing the hair, delivering a knee strike to the solar plexus, and pushing the attacker away. Note that the knee strike should be to the solar plexus instead of the face, because striking to the face or head with the top of the thigh could cause tori to have a painful, disabling charley horse from the blow to his own quadriceps muscles on the top of his leg.

Photo 11

Photo 12

Photo 13

Photo 14

Photo 15

Photo 16

Exercise 8 trains you to defend against an up-close sucker punch, or uppercut, by an attacker, and involves the use of *kaiten nage* (circle throw). Tori blocks downward with his *tegatana* (or sword hand) and simultaneously performs a palm heel strike to kake's nose. Tori's lead hand then goes around the attacker's neck, using the knife-edge of the hand against the back of the neck, and his lower hand turns over to grab kake's striking arm. Tori then pivots, and, dropping to his knee, moves his arms around in a circular fashion, throwing kake. He then stands and pivots back to end in T-dachi stance, completing the exercise.

In Photos 17 through 21, as the attacker attempts to strike tori with a right uppercut, tori simultaneously blocks downward with his left hand, and delivers a palm heel strike to kake's nose with his right hand. Tori then places his right hand behind the neck of kake (using a tegatana), securing his right wrist with his left hand, turns, and drops to one knee while throwing the attacker to his rear.

Photo 17

Photo 18

Photo 19

Photo 20

Photo 21

Exercise 5A, like Exercise 5, is also against a rear inside grab. Tori turns with the grab, with his arm held firmly to open up the attacker. He swings his arm up and around to the outside in a large circle, finishing with his palm pointing down. He then steps through with his back leg, pushing downward with the same hand, and pulling upward with the other. Tori completes the exercise by turning back to the front, and ending in T-dachi.

In Photos 22 through 25, as tori is grabbed from the rear again with an inside grab, tori quickly turns and slides away slightly, keeping his right arm firm. He then wraps his arm around to the outside, and under kake's grabbing arm, and grabs kake by the belt from the top. Tori then steps through with his left foot, pulling up on kake's belt, and pushes down with his left hand, finally dropping kake to his back.

Photo 22

Photo 23

Photo 24

Photo 25

In Exercise 6A, tori again turns because of an outside attack from the rear, and, keeping his right arm firm, simultaneously strikes to the ribs of kake. Continuing, tori steps in with his back leg, behind the lead leg of kake, and strikes kake's neck with his elbow. Tori then pushes down and rearward with his arm, hand-dropping the attacker, and turns back to the front to finish the exercise.

In Photos 26 through 30, tori, grabbed from the rear in an outside grab, turns quickly to his left, keeping his left arm firm, and strikes to the ribs of the attacker. He then secures the attacker's arm with his left hand, steps in, and delivers an elbow atemi to the head or ribs of the attacker. Finally, he pushes backward with his right arm, and forward with his right knee (which has been placed directly behind the left knee of the attacker) and drops the attacker to the rear.

Photo 26

Photo 27

Photo 28

Photo 29

Photo 30

Exercise 7A teaches defense against a front kick from the outside. Tori steps forward with his lead leg, and his lead arm swings forward, little-finger side of the hand leading, as he withdraws his opposite arm the same distance. He then pivots his lead foot and steps through, lifting his back arm and striking the biceps of the arm swinging forward. He drops to his knee, and strikes downward with a tegatana to kake's groin. He places his hands on the floor, and with his lead leg, kicks to the upper body of the downed attacker. Returning his kicking leg, he ends in *hantachi* (half-kneeling stance).

In Photos 31 through 35, tori defends against kake's front kick from the outside by deflecting his arm as he steps through, dropping the attacker to the rear. As the attacker's head comes up from the strike to the groin, tori finishes the technique with a kick to kake's head.

Photo 31

Photo 32

Photo 33

Photo 34

Photo 35

Exercise 8A, like Exercise 8, is a defense against a close-in strike to the head. As kake strikes to tori's head, tori drops to his knee with his leading arm raised to guard his head and his back arm striking to kake's groin. Tori then pulls back with the striking hand, and his back arm strikes to kake's groin. Tori then pulls back with the striking hand, and pushes forward with his lead arm, bringing his arm around in a full circle, ending with a hammer fist strike to kake's groin. Tori then stands up to T-dachi stance, and steps back one step to end in T-dachi.

In Photos 36 through 38, as the attacker steps in to strike at his head, tori drops to one knee and executes a groin strike and grab with his right hand. He then pulls outward with his right hand, and pushes backwards with his left, dropping kake to the rear, and finishing with another strike to kake's groin.

Note that these exercises should be performed to both sides when practicing them. Perform them slowly and carefully so as not to accidentally injure your partner. The photographs of the Bunkai applications should clarify any misunderstanding you might have as to the meaning of the exercises, and the exact movements involved. Study them carefully.

Photo 36

Photo 37

Photo 38

Chapter 3

Nidan-Gi Waza

Suwari waza (sitting)	Translation	Principle
Matsuba dori	Pine-needle technique	Thumb break
Te kagami	Hand mirror	The grip or pin
Ude osae dori	Shoulder pin technique	Nidan pressing control, wrist bind
Mune osae dori	Chest, lapel grab art	Nidan pressing control, wrist bind
Konoha gaeshi	Turning of the leaf	Konoha gaeshi
Riote konoha gaeshi	Two-handed turning of the leaf	Konoha gaeshi
Uchi komi dori	Downward strike art	Nidan pressing control, wrist bind
Mae riote osae dori	Front two-handed grab and kick defense	Nidan pressing control, wrist bind
Isu osae dori	Chair defense technique	Nidan pressing control, wrist bind
Tachi waza (standing)	**Translation**	**Principle**
Tachi matsuba dori	Standing pine-needle technique	Thumb break

Tachi waza (standing)	Translation	Principle
Maki komi	Wrapping inside art	Maki komi
Katate osae aya dori	Woven-art technique	Aya dori
Mune konoha gaeshi	Chest, lapel grab art	Konoha gaeshi
Tachi te kagami	Standing hand mirror	The grip or pin
Tachi ude osae dori	Standing sleeve grab, nidan wrist bind	Nidan pressing control, wrist bind
Tachi mune osae dori	Standing chest-grab defense	Nidan pressing control, wrist bind
Mae niho nage	Front two-directional throw	Niho nage

Tachi waza (standing)	Translation	Principle
Ushiro niho nage	Rear two-directional throw	Niho nage
Aku shu	Nidan handshake technique	Konoha gaeshi
Kaban dori	Nidan briefcase technique	Konoha gaeshi
Futari nin dori	Two-man defense while sitting	Konoha gaeshi
Shuto jime, tegatana shime	Nidan sword-hand lock or squeeze	Shuto jime

SUWARI WAZA: KNEELING TECHNIQUES

In *matsuba dori,* the pine-needle break (Photos 39 through 43), kake grabs tori by both wrists. Then tori swings one hand up to the outside and brings the other hand over to secure the grip, right hand palm facing outward. Tori then rotates his right hand inward, places the tegatana over the left wrist of kake, and, cutting downward with his little finger and pushing forward at the same time, causes kake to submit in great pain. This particular technique, when performed correctly, simultaneously locks the joints of the wrist, elbow, and shoulder, immobilizing the arm completely. The close-up in Photo 43 shows the proper hand position.

Photo 39

Photo 40

Photo 41

Photo 42

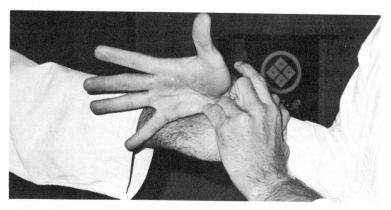

Photo 43

In *te kagami,* the hand mirror (Photos 44 through 47), the technique begins with a wrist twist, which causes kake to fall to the side. Tori then grips the fingers of kake's right hand with his left hand, and grips kake's wrist with his right hand. He then pulls upward and toward himself, and finishes with a pin against the base of the ear (mastoid process) with the middle knuckle of his right index finger. He pivots around during this action to secure kake's head firmly against his knee to prevent escape, and leans down with his full weight pressing down on the mastoid process with his knuckle atemi.

Photo 44

Photo 45

Photo 46

Photo 47

In *ude osae dori,* the nidan wrist bind (Photos 48 through 51), tori is grabbed by kake on his right upper sleeve. Tori secures kake's hand after delivering a metsubushi to kake, and pins the hand firmly against his arm, so that kake cannot let loose. Tori then brings his arm forward, up and around from the outside, and over the grabbing wrist of kake. Relaxing his shoulder and letting his arm drop, tori applies painful pressure downward and forward against kake's wrist, elbow, and shoulder joints, taking him to the ground and submission. Use caution when learning this technique. Do not apply pressure downward with the arm too fast or too strongly. Kake will not be able to react quickly enough, and you could break his wrist or elbow.

Photo 48

Photo 49

Photo 50

Photo 51

In *mune osae dori,* the chest grab and nidan wrist bind (Photos 52 through 55), when grabbed on the chest by kake, tori executes simultaneously a strike to the elbow and a metsubushi strike to kake's face. He then secures and pins kake's wrist to his chest, and with the bone at the base of his left index finger, applies pressure upward and forward against the wrist of kake (on the heart meridian), turning kake's wrist over to a vertical position. Sliding his left hand into place with the fingers over his right hand, tori causes a slight bend in the wrist of kake, while applying pressure inward and downward toward kake's belt, forcing him to the ground and into submission.

Photo 52

Photo 53

Photo 54

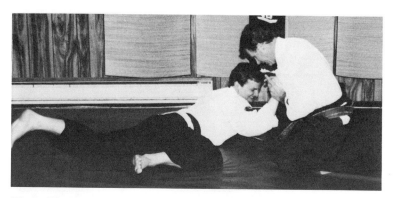

Photo 55

In *konoha gaeshi*, the turning of the leaf (Photos 56 through 61), when grabbed on the chest by the left hand, tori secures the free right hand of kake, and immediately delivers a metsubushi strike to kake's face. Placing his thumb on the back of kake's right hand and gripping firmly with his fingers, he turns it upward, and locks the wrist. Pushing his elbow straight back and downward, he causes kake to fall to the side. Keeping his grip on the hand, tori takes out the slack in kake's wrist, places it at a 45-degree angle, keeps his own wrist firm, and cuts downward with the little finger of his left hand, pinning kake to the ground in sharp pain until submission. Photo 61 shows the close-up view of the proper hand grip position.

Photo 56

Photo 57

Photo 58

Photo 59

Photo 60

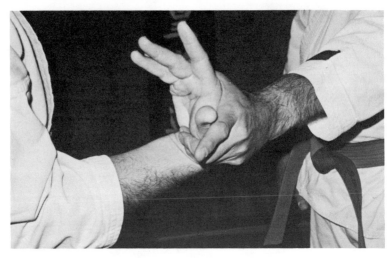

Photo 61

Riote konoha gaeshi, the two-handed turning of the leaf (Photos 62 through 65), is similar to konoha gaeshi, except that in this case tori takes the initiative by grabbing both of kake's hands and applying konoha gaeshi to both at the same time. Tori then has the option of throwing kake in any direction, left, right, or to the rear, finishing the technique in the same manner as described for konoha gaeshi.

Photo 62

Photo 63

Photo 64

Photo 65

Uchi komi dori, nidan's powerful downward strike (Photos 66 through 68), teaches that, as kake strikes downward with his left hand, tori should deflect the strike from below, deflecting the strike with his right hand above the elbow of kake, and use his left hand to guide and redirect the left hand of the attacker. Using just the tegatana, and not grabbing the wrist, tori pushes his right hand toward kake's face, and moves his left hand in a circular motion, unbalancing kake. He then brings his left hand back, fingers overlapping the right hand, and applies the nidan wrist bind, leaning slightly forward, and driving kake to the ground in pain.

Photo 66

Photo 67

Photo 68

Mae riote osae dori, the front two-handed grab and kick defense (Photos 69 through 72), involves the principle of *niho/shiho nage* (two-/four-directional throw). As tori sits in seiza, kake grabs him by the wrists, pulls him, and attempts to kick him. Tori blocks the kick with the back of kake's left hand against his own knee, and then steps through with his right foot, applying a painful wristlock bind, causing kake to turn away. He then pivots to his left, lifting his arm and making sure his left hand is gripping the wrist of kake, takes kake down to the rear with *gakun* (a grip that pulls with the little finger and pushes with the thumb), and finishes with a knee pin and pressure-point hold until kake submits.

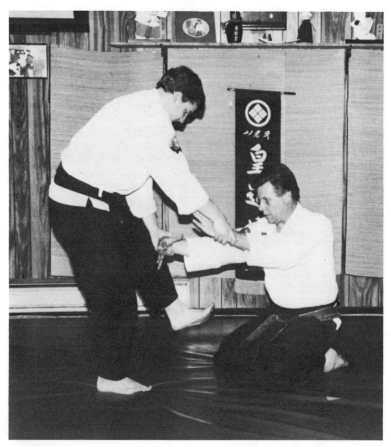

Photo 69

Photo 70

Photo 71

Photo 72

In *isu osae dori,* the nidan chair defense technique, version A (Photos 73 through 75), as tori is sitting in his chair, kake grabs him by the wrists and attempts to pull him out of the chair. Tori relaxes his arms, and applies the *yoko katate osae dori* wristlock, also known as *suimon,* or the floodgate lock. Tori uses the lock to bring the attacker back, around, and down to the front, taking him to the ground and pinning him behind his ear, with kake's head on tori's foot. Tori then uses the lock to bring the attacker back, around, and down to the front, taking him to the ground, and pinning him behind his ear, with kake's head on tori's foot. Tori then uses his toes, bent upward, to apply atemi to the side of kake's head, without moving from his chair.

Photo 73

Photo 74

Photo 75

Version B of isu osae dori (Photos 76 through 79), starts with the same type of attack, but this time tori steps up from the chair in front of kake, and applies the suimon lock, dropping his hips. Straightening up to apply pressure, tori then pivots to his left, walks kake back to the chair, and completes the technique with a wristlock, applying pressure to the side of kake's neck with his free hand.

A modified version of isu osae dori is more severe in its application. After the tori steps out of the chair, he pivots and, instead of walking kake back to the chair and sitting him down, he takes kake down in place, striking his head directly onto the seat of the chair.

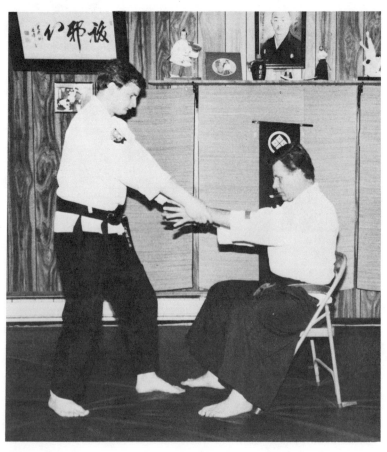

Photo 76

Photo 77

Photo 78

Photo 79

TACHI WAZA: STANDING TECHNIQUES

In *tachi matsuba dori,* the nidan standing pine-needle break and control (Photos 80 through 82), when tori is grabbed by both wrists, he steps back slightly with his left foot into T-dachi, and swings his right arm outward and inward, securing kake's left hand to his own right wrist. Tori then rotates his right hand, palm inward, over the upper side of kake's wrist, and, keeping his right arm in close to his body, cuts downward with his right little finger, and pushes toward kake's belt, forcing kake back and down into submission.

Photo 80

Photo 81

Photo 82

Maki komi is the nidan wrapping technique as shown in Photos 83 through 88. As kake grabs the left upper arm of tori and strikes with his left hand, tori blocks the strike with a tegatana strike to the biceps of kake's striking arm, and simultaneously pins kake's right hand to his upper arm by use of his left forearm. With his left palm pointing forward, tori rotates his left forearm and hand downward, as if touching his own stomach with the little finger of his left hand. Tori then bends forward, placing the ulnar bone of his left forearm and hand downward, as if touching his own stomach with the little finger of his left hand. Tori then bends forward, placing the ulnar bone of his left forearm against the radial bone of the attacker's arm, putting kake in considerable pain and causing him to lose his balance. Tori then continues pulling downward as he steps back with his left foot, and turns to the left, dropping kake to the floor. He can then finish the pin, thrusting the big toe of his right foot or the thumb of his right hand into kake's armpit nerve area. The last photo in this series (88) shows a close-up view of the proper arm placement when rolling the ulnar bone against the radial bone of kake.

Photo 83

Photo 84

Photo 85

Photo 86

Photo 87

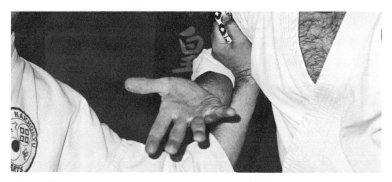

Photo 88

In *katate osae aya dori,* the woven-art technique (Photos 89 through 93), kake grabs the right hand of tori and attempts to strike tori with his right hand. Tori steps back slightly and out of the line to his right, and swings his right arm outward and up, securing the grabbing hand with his left. The fingers overlap this point, and this is what gives this technique the name of woven art. If desired, tori can deliver an atemi kick to kake's rib or side thigh area, and, applying a wrist bind to the grabbing hand, force the attacker down in submission. The last photo in this series (93) shows a close-up of the proper hand position for tori. You should keep the elbow high, and push in toward the shoulder of kake with the little finger of the right hand.

Photo 89

Photo 90

Photo 91

Photo 92

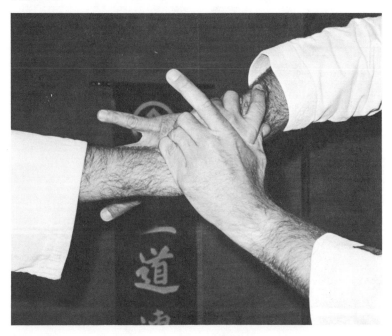

Photo 93

Mune konoha gaeshi, the chest grab and turning of the leaf (Photos 94 and 95), shows what will happen when kake grabs tori on the chest with his left hand. Tori grabs the free right hand of kake and simultaneously performs metsubushi to kake's face as he turns the hand upward, unbalancing kake. Tori then steps forward with his left foot, pushing kake's elbow downward, dropping him to the rear. Tori retains his grip and finishes with the pin as shown in the kneeling waza, konoha gaeshi. This particular waza also has two other versions: a version with the kake striking after the grab, and a version wherein the hand that has grabbed the lapel is used for the konoha gaeshi pin and takedown.

Photo 94

Photo 95

In *tachi te kagami,* the standing hand mirror technique (Photos 96 through 98), when grabbed on both hands, tori performs te kagami waza, flexing his wrists up, turning his left palm toward his face like a hand mirror, and grabbing the underside of kake's hand. Then twisting kake's hand, tori throws kake. But after kake is thrown, tori makes the final pin, as in the *suwari* version, and places his right foot under the head of kake, pressing down with his full weight on the pressure point of kake's mastoid process with the middle knuckle of his right index finger. Note: This is a very painful pressure-point pin and can cause drowsiness; it can even result in loss of consciousness if too much pressure is applied or the pressure is held for too long. Exercise caution!

Photo 96

Photo 97

Photo 98

Tachi ude osae dori, the standing sleeve grab and nidan wrist bind (Photos 99 through 102), shows that when kake grabs tori on the left sleeve, after executing metsubushi strike to his face, tori pins kake's hand to his arm. Tori then pushes forward with his right arm, taking kake backwards and off balance, and preventing kake's striking back with his free hand. After applying the nidan wrist bind and forcing kake down, tori steps back with his left leg, keeping pressure on kake's wrist, elbow, and shoulder joint, and pins kake to the floor in submission. This is a very painful pin and lock, and should be performed with care in practice!

Photo 99

Photo 100

Photo 101

Photo 102

In *tachi mune osae dori,* the standing chest grab defense (Photos 103 through 106), kake first grabs tori on the lapel with his left hand and attempts to strike tori with his right hand. Tori executes a metsubushi strike, and turns slightly away, raising his left arm to protect his head. Tori then secures the left hand to his chest, and turning it over with his right hand, applies the downward pressure of the lock, forcing kake back and downward. He finally steps back with his left foot, retaining the pin on his chest, and takes kake to submission. For this final pin, tori should use his chest and body weight to apply pressure downward against the wrist.

Photo 103

Photo 104

Photo 105

Photo 106

In *mae niho nage,* the front two-directional throw (Photos 107 through 110), tori, grabbed by one hand, avoids the strike attempted by kake by executing the suimon lock against kake's wrist. (To make this lock successful, tori must fully extend the grabbing arm.) Tori then steps through with his right leg while securing kake's grabbing hand with his own left hand, pivots to his left, and drops to his right knee, bringing kake down, and finishing with a controlling pin against kake's mastoid process.

Photo 107

Photo 108

Photo 109

Photo 110

In *uchi komi dori,* the nidan defense against an overhand blow (Photos 111 through 114), as kake strikes a downward blow against tori, tori deflects the blow upward and to the rear, using tegatana. With a circular motion of his left hand, he forces kake down. He then brings his right hand to his left, and applies the nidan level lock, forcing kake downward. He then steps back, and continues the pressure by applying a gakun grip to the wrist, forcing kake into submission. It is important to apply the gakun action while taking kake to the floor, and not just attempt to pull him down to the floor with your weight or strength.

Photo 111

Photo 112

Photo 113

Photo 114

In using *ushiro niho nage,* the rear two-directional throw (Photos 115 through 118), when kake grabs both wrists and attempts to pull tori, tori first goes with the pulling action and steps to the outside of kake's right foot. Then, dropping down, tori applies the suimon lock and continues his pivot to the right. Applying the gakun grip, he drops kake to his rear and finishes with the pin and control, using his knee against kake's ribs to prevent possible rollover or escape of the attacker.

Photo 115

Photo 116

Photo 117

Photo 118

Aku shu, the nidan handshake technique (Photos 119 through 122), is a konoha gaeshi principle. As the two are shaking hands, kake attempts to overpower tori, or squeeze his hand too hard. Tori places his left hand on the back of kake's, and steps in with his left foot while executing an elbow-atemi strike to kake's face. Tori then forces kake back and down by applying the konoha gaeshi (turning of the leaf) principle and pins him using the lock described earlier for konoha gaeshi.

Photo 119

Photo 120

Photo 121

Photo 122

In the first version of *kaban dori,* the nidan briefcase technique (Photos 123 through 126), as tori is walking and carrying his briefcase, kake approaches from the front and attempts to grab the case away from tori. As he does this, tori allows the case to swing backward in the direction of kake, and then pivots to his left, swinging the case upward and unbalancing kake. Tori finally secures the grabbing hand with his own right hand, applying the konoha gaeshi principle, and forces kake down to his rear, removing the briefcase and finishing with the pin.

Photo 123

Photo 124

Photo 125

Photo 126

The second version of kaban dori (Photos 127 through 130), shows another avenue of defense when tori is carrying a briefcase. As tori is walking with the briefcase, he is approached from the rear in the same direction. As kake attempts to steal the briefcase, tori lets the case swing forward. Tori then turns left and swings the case back into the face of the thief. Again he secures kake's grabbing hand with his right, and applying the konoha gaeshi principle, drives kake down to the rear, and finishes with a pin to submission.

Photo 127

Photo 128

Photo 129

Photo 130

Futari nin dori is the nidan two-man defense while sitting technique (Photos 131 through 134). From *hantachi* (the half-kneeling stance), tori is grabbed by both arms from the sides by two men. He relaxes his arms and pulls first one, then the other man in toward him, using the little finger side of his hand. He swings his hand back and then forward, and applies the *shuto jime* lock, forcing both men to the ground, face down. Securing both wrists on his thighs momentarily, tori switches hands and secures the wrists of both assailants, crossing their arms, and pinning them both with a painful shodan pin to submission.

Photo 131

Photo 132

Photo 133

Photo 134

The *shuto jime* or *tegatana shime,* the nidan sword-hand lock or squeeze (Photos 135 through 138), begins as tori is grabbed by both hands. In response, tori opens his hands and swings them outward. Then, rotating his hands inward as in matsuba dori (shown earlier), he keeps them about a shoulder's width apart and applies the lock on both of kake's wrists at the same time. He slowly lowers both hands toward kake's belt, forcing kake to break his balance because of the pain, and finally, pushes kake back and away. Note: This waza may also be performed when grabbed by two hands on one arm.

Photo 135

Photo 136

Photo 137

Photo 138

Chapter 4

Origins and Applications of Hakkoryu Waza

The exact time of emergence of the empty-handed techniques is difficult to pinpoint with any true precision. Schools and techniques of the Daitoryu can trace their lineage back some five-hundred-plus years, and document the use of certain techniques contained in Daitoryu aiki-jujutsu. The techniques of the Daitoryu and other aiki-jujutsu-related schools evolved almost concurrently with the schools of kenjutsu, or sword fighting. Although the schools of the sword were many and varied, it is naive to think that none of these schools recognized the eventuality of having to defend oneself unarmed in battle or various other confrontations, and schools obviously developed several techniques to be used in unarmed combative encounters. Based on this premise, with the demise of the samurai and his authority to carry on his person two swords *(daisho),* and the resultant "civilizing" of Japan during the Tokugawa Shogunate of the Edo period (1603-1868), those who were masters of the sword had no outlet for their skills other than to teach a few students, or as special retainers to the emperor. It was during this period of time that the skills of aiki-jujutsu began to be refined and developed into a system of unarmed self-defense, much of which was based totally on techniques once used in defense with a sword or against a sword. These formidable masters of kenjutsu would not and could not let their skills, art, and knowledge die because of a dictum of the emperor. Thus their only legal outlet for preserving their knowledge and passing on their skills was through the refined development of the unarmed arts of jujutsu and aiki-jujutsu.

As is illustrated in this chapter, many of the unarmed techniques of jujutsu are derived directly from similar or identical applications with the sword. In Hakkoryu, techniques such as *tachi ate,* niho/shiho nage, te kagami, uchi komi dori, and maki komi can be easily shown to have been derived from the kenjutsu skills of the older schools of the sword. It is for this reason that the traditional schools of jujutsu refer to the tegatana (sword-hand strike) rather than the *shuto,* or knife-hand strike, of karate. The side of the hand is considered just as deadly as the cutting edge of a Japanese sword, and in the execution of waza, the student who does not keep this fact uppermost in mind has lost sight of the origins of a waza and its application. Hence, the student's technique will always be lacking in effectiveness. The beauty of an aiki-jujutsu based art is not just in its form and waza or in the potential destructiveness of a technique, but also in its *elegance* of execution. A true practitioner will defeat his opponent(s) with minimal effort, total control, and effortlessness. Elegance by itself is hollow, and victory, with brutality and vengeance, is at best crude. But victory with elegance, *zanshin* (perfect posture), and the positive image of power and control is a sight to behold.

The mastering of waza is different than the mastering of technique. The former will be the result of developing a conditioned reflex, whereas the latter is merely a rational thought or movement. One must progress from the rational thought or reaction to the level of a conditioned proper reflex, to even the level of *mushin,* or "no mind"—no planned thought, no planned reaction, just action when needed. For example, a professional baseball player would never be able to hit a ball effectively if he had to plan when to hit or swing at a pitch. He must relax, think of nothing, and when it's time, merely hit the ball. Any thought given over to timing of the swing, which pitch to swing at, where to hit, etc., will stop his "no mind" reaction, and cause him to miss. In a baseball game, this may result in a strikeout, a bad hit, a double play, or whatever. However, in a fight, such a reaction may result in injury or even death. As Miyamoto Mushashi (1584–1645) points out in his famous work, *Book of Five Rings,* the swordsman does not think of cutting and he does not think of killing. He merely cuts—unlike baseball, in a life/death struggle, you get no second chance. The "inning" is over with one strike. If you make the wrong move, if you delay, if you have any doubt about its effectiveness, you could be dead! Therefore, one should always practice in earnest, with a sense of danger, and an intensity of concentration. Never practice halfway, or quit on a technique. This type of training will result in the same type of response when needed. Just as the master swordsman cuts without thinking, the *jujutsuka* must react without thinking. The reaction of the body in mushin now totally overcomes the mind, and you just react. The waza of nidan-gi will begin to allow this to happen.

The philosophy of Hakkoryu is strongly founded on the belief of the precept *ju yoku go o seisu,* or mildness governs more than anger. As one continues to train in the arts of Hakkoryu, if his heart is true and he follows the guidance of the Soke and the transmission of the *okuden* (secret techniques) of the higher levels, he will begin to develop the quality of *ishin denshin,* or thought transference, which is the ability to comprehend the intentions of another without speaking. To attain this level, the practitioner must live his or her life in truth *(shinjitsu ichiro),* and be true to his or her own heart. When this is attained, the beauty of *yo wa i ki,* i.e., being with peace and harmony, will be the end result.

One story that comes to mind at this time is that of Dai Soke Okuyama when he attended a graduation party at the Hombu for newly elevated shihan. After the party, Soke and the new shihan were sitting around a small table and talking. It was obvious that the new shihan were totally engrossed in Soke's every word and gesture, and I'm sure his actions were his way of saying there is an explanation for everything, and that to live one's life in the true spirit, one must not be deceived by appearances. While the shihan were pouring sake for the Soke and each other, a few drops of sake fell on the table surface. Soke caught sight of the drops and asked everyone to be still and silent. Then, as Soke concentrated his full energy on the drops, the drops began to move. Everyone was amazed. They knew he was a man of formidable abilities, but to move the motionless drops of sake with just his concentration was quite a feat. Everyone applauded at the feat. Soke just smiled and pointed at his knee, which, unbeknownst to the others at the table, was against the leg of the small table. All he truly did was move the table slightly with his knee to make the drops of sake move. He had tricked them all, and taught a valuable lesson at the same time. Don't imagine a situation, but take it for what it is. The eyes and body can be deceived, but the mind should overcome the outward appearances *(ken),* and see to the truth of the situation *(kan).* The Dai Soke had struck again in his own inimitable way. As you train, try to recapture the innocence and peace of mind you had when a child of four or five years of age—ready to learn as much as you can, and happy with yourself. This is the spirit of Hakkoryu.

APPLICATIONS OF WAZA

If an individual was so bold as to grab the handle of a samurai's sword, the samurai could very easily have used te kagami to disengage the aggressor, throw him, and finish him off, from either the sitting position or the standing position. This is illustrated in Photos 139 through 143.

At the nidan level, the use of ude osae dori, the empty-handed arm bar, might well have been derived from the use of the samurai's *wakizashi* or katana (his swords) as he was attacked or grabbed on the sleeve. Using the sword in the same manner as the open-hand technique, the defender can force the aggressor to the ground under the direct pressure of the blade (Photos 144 through 147). In this series, as he draws the sword from the scabbard, the samurai cuts the underside of the attacker's arm, then comes across from the

Photo 139

Photo 140

Photo 141

Photo 142

Photo 143

Photo 144

Photo 145

Photo 146

Photo 147

outside, laying the blade across his neck and forcing him to the ground.

It is quite universally accepted that the defense illustrated in this series (Photos 148 through 150) was the origin of *mae niho nage,* an effective and popular waza of the aikijutsu arts. This waza is a defense against the overhead attack with a sword, and removes the sword from the attacker's hands, finishing him off with his own sword.

Maki komi is a wrapping or winding technique which could also very easily have been derived from a sequence, as illustrated in Photos 151 through 155. Rather than using the hard ulnar bone of the forearm as is done in maki komi, the even harder handle of the sword *(tsuka)* could be used to defeat the attacker, causing excruciating pain, and taking him to the ground.

Matsuba dori, the pine-needle break, might very possibly have been used as a defense against the grab of the sword handle, with the practitioner first breaking (dislocating) the thumb of the grabbing hand, then felling the attacker with the sword-hand lock, and finally controlling from the

Photo 148

Photo 149

Photo 150

Photo 151

Photo 152

Photo 153

Photo 154

Photo 155

outside of the wrist (Photos 156 and 157). The colorful name for this technique was given by Dai Soke Okuyama, and is quite common to many of the waza of Hakkoryu. The pine-needle break illustrates the idea that the thumb is as easily snapped and broken as are the brittle needles on a pine tree.

The technique *aya dori* was so named by Dai Soke Okuyama because, when done properly, the hand positions and overlapping fingers resemble a piece of woven straw; thus the name aya dori, or woven-art technique.

The waza te kagami (hand mirror) receives its name because the first movement of the waza is like that of one looking at a small mirror in one's hand.

Konoha gaeshi, called *kote* gaeshi (wrist reversal) in some related aiki arts, means "turning of the leaf" in Hakkoryu and was so named by Dai Soke Okuyama. Emphasis is not on a strong outside twist of the attacker's wrist, but on folding the wrist back directly into the elbow, making it much more difficult to resist, and causing a sharp immediate pain, as opposed to a dull pain and possible break when using an outside twist such as in *kote gaeshi.*

The primary principles of nidan-gi are thus illustrated in these above-mentioned waza, plus others, namely shuto jime, or tegatana shime; nidan osae dori, niho nage, and maki komi. These are the primary principles *(gokui)* of nidan-gi waza.

APPLICATIONS OF THE PRINCIPLES
OF NIDAN-GI

In the following series of illustrations, the applications of some of the principles are illustrated in situations one might encounter outside of the dojo. In the first series, tori is seated at a table when he is approached and grabbed by kake, who attempts to strike him. Tori negates the strike using the suimon wristlock principle, then steps out of his chair, applying niho nage with wristlock to force kake back and down, striking his head on the chair (Photos 158 through 162).

The next series (Photos 163 through 167) again shows the use of niho nage. Tori is walking past his automobile

Photo 156

Photo 157

Photo 158

Photo 159

Photo 160

Photo 161

Photo 162

Photo 163

Photo 164

Photo 165

Photo 166

Photo 167

when kake jumps out from the front and grabs him by the arm, attempting to pull him or assault him. Tori uses hakko dori to negate the pull, then applies the wristlock of niho nage, and finishes by slamming kake down on the hood of the car, again thwarting the mugger's attack.

In photos 168 through 170, while walking and carrying his briefcase, tori is approached from the rear by kake who attempts to steal his briefcase out of his hand. Tori immediately goes with the grab, swings the case up and back into kake's face, and grasps his wrist for the application of konoha gaeshi principle. He secures his wrist, and pushing his elbow down, force kake to the rear, finishing with a controlling wristlock.

Photo 168

Photo 169

Photo 170

In the last series (Photos 171 through 173), tori is walking and carrying an object in one hand, when he is attacked from the rear by kake. Without having to drop or lose the object he is carrying, tori negates the grab by opening his hand and applying the principle of shuto jime to kake, forcing him down to the ground in submission, and finishing the technique.

Photo 171

Photo 172

Photo 173

In closing, the attitude of the Hakkoryu practitioner should be to emulate the attitude of Hakkoryu's founder in his approach to life and his fellowman. He must strive to develop patience *(nintai)*, expand his efforts *(doryoku)*, develop belief and love *(shin-ai)*, maintain an energetic mental attitude *(konjyo)*, and temper his actions with mercy *(jihi)*. Without these qualities, one cannot develop the *Hakko Seishin*, or true spirit, of Hakkoryu.

Mastery is not something that strikes in an instant,
        like a thunderbolt;
But a gathering power that moves through time,
        like weather.
Soseki

Appendix

GLOSSARY OF JAPANESE TERMS

Agete, sagete	*Lift, lower*
Ago	*Chin*
Aku shu	*Handshake defense*
Atemi	*Strike to vital point of the body*
Aya dori	*Woven-art technique*
Bugai	*Martial arts*
Bunkai	*Doing an exercise with another person*
Chotto matte kudasai	*Please wait*
Chumoku, kiotsuke!	*Attention!*
Daitoryu	*Style of aiki-jujutsu, Great Eastern school*
Dame	*Bad, not good*
Dozo yoroshiku	*Please do me a favor*
Futari nin dori	*Sitting defense against two men*
Gaijin	*Foreigner*
Gakun	*A grip that pulls with the little finger and pushes with the thumb*
Gomen-nasai	*Excuse me*
Ha-i, i-ie	*Yes, no*
Ha-i, wakarimashita	*Yes, I understand*

Hajime-mashite	*Begin*
Hakko no kamae	*Stance of Hakkoryu*
Hana	*Nose*
Hanasu	*Let go*
Hantachi	*Half-kneeling stance, with one knee raised*
Hara	*The abdominal area, containing the vital organs*
Hombu	*Hakkoryu headquarters in Japan*
Itai	*It hurts!*
Jikideshi	*Student and direct disciple of the soke*
Kaiden shidan	*Master-appointed disicple of soke, holder of the deepest mysteries of the ryu*
Kake	*Aggressor, attacker*
Kamae	*Stance*
Kata	*Shoulder*
Keiko, renshu	*Exercise, practice or workout*
Kenjutsu	*Sword fighting art*
Kiritsu, tate	*Stand up*
Ko	*Technician*
Koho igaku shiatsu	*Imperial way of finger pressure massage*
Konoha gaeshi	*Turning of the leaf*
Kyusho	*Vital point*
Maki komi	*Wrapping technique*
Mata	*Thigh*
Matsuba dori	*Pine-needle break*
Me	*Eye*
Metsubushi	*Open-handed strike to face with back and nails of fingers; literally: to blind by throwing ashes in the eyes*
Mijikaku, nagaku	*Shorter, longer*
Mo-ichido	*Once more*
Mudansha	*Below black belt level*
Mune osae dori	*Chest, lapel grab defense*

Mushin	*No mind; no planned thought or reaction, just action when needed*
Nidan	*Second degree black belt*
Nigiru, tsukamu	*Grasp, seize*
Niho nage	*Two-directional throw*
Ogenki-desunka?	*How are you?*
Oi zuki	*Thrusting punch*
Okuden	*The hidden, secret techniques of Hakkoryu*
Osu, hiku	*Push, pull*
Oya-yubi	*Thumb*
Renshi shihan	*Senior master, brother of soke*
Renshu, keiko hajime	*Begin the workout*
Renshu, keiko owari	*Stop the workout*
San Dai Kichu	*Highest rank in Hakkoryu jujutsu, literally, Three Great Foundation Pillars*
Sandan	*Third degree black belt*
Sayonara	*Goodbye*
Seiken	*Forefist (calcified, fused knuckles)*
Seiretsu, seiton	*Array, put in order*
Seiza	*Sit straight, formal kneeling position*
Senpenbanka	*Stance of innumerable changes, literally, one thousand times ten thousand positions*
Shiatsu	*Massage*
Shichidan	*Seventh degree black belt*
Shihan	*Master, instructor*
Shihan menkyo	*Licensed rank of Hakkoryu artists*
Shiho nage	*Four-direction throw*
Shinden ni rei	*Bow, salute the shrine*
Shodan	*First degree black belt*
Shoshinsha	*New, uninitiated student*
Shuto jime	*Sword-hand lock principle*

Soke	*Grandmaster*
Sonkei	*Respect*
Sonomama!	*Don't move!*
Suimon	*The floodgate lock*
Suki	*Gap*
Sumimasen	*I'm sorry (for what I've just done)*
Suwari	*Kneeling*
Tachi ate	*Standing strike*
Tachi-rei, za-rei	*Standing bow, sitting bow*
Tai sabaki	*Body positioning, movement*
Tanden	*Within the* hara, *3 to 5 inches below the navel*
Tegatana	*Sword hand strike*
Teiji-dachi	*T-stance*
Te kagami	*Hand mirror (defensive hand grip) technique*
Tekiyo	*Application of a technique*
Tekubi	*Wrist*
Tomare!	*Stop!*
Tori	*Defender, he who applies the technique*
Tsumasaki	*Tiptoe*
Uchi komi dori	*Downward-strike defense*
Ude	*Arm*
Ude osae dori	*Sleeve-grab, shoulder-pin defense*
Ue, shite	*Upper part, lower part*
Wakibara	*Side of the body*
Waza	*Technique*
Yoko men uchi	*Roundhouse strike to the head*
Yondan	*Fourth degree black belt*
Yudansha	*Black-belt level students*
Zanshin	*Perfect posture*
Zen-in tate	*Stand up*

Other books by Dennis G. Palumbo,
Kaiden Shihan San Dai Kichi:

The Secrets of Hakkoryu Jujutsu: Shodan Tactics

If you have further questions about the techniques and/or
training available in Hakkoryu Jujutsu, please do not hesitate
to contact the author either through Paladin Press, or at his
dojo:

Dennis G. Palumbo
Hakkoryu Martial Arts Federation
12028F East Mississippi Avenue
Aurora, Colorado 80012